Gods and Heroes

in the

Athenian Agora

Relief of the Cave of Pan.
Second half of the 4th century B.C.

AMERICAN SCHOOL
OF CLASSICAL STUDIES
AT ATHENS
1980

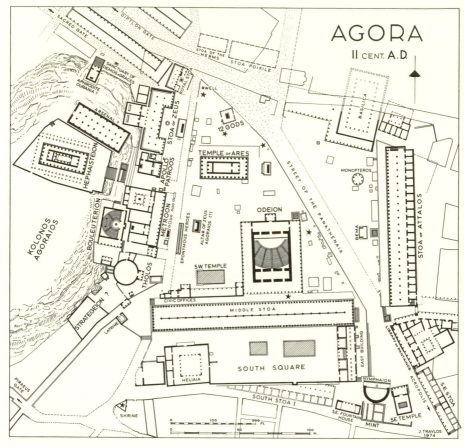

1. Plan of the Agora in the 2nd century after Christ, showing the principal cult locations.

GODS		HEROES
Aphrodite	Hera	Aiakos
Apollo	Herakles	Daughters of Leos
Ares	Hermes	Epitegios
Artemis	Hestia	The Eponymous Heroes
Asklepios	Mithras	Eurysakes
Athena	Mother of the Gods	Strategos
Demeter	Pan	Theseus
Dionysos	Poseidon	The Tyrannicides
Egyptian Gods	The Twelve Gods	
Hekate	Zeus	
Hephaistos		

THE ATHENIAN AGORA, in addition to being the political, administrative, commercial, and social center of town, was also very much the focus of religious life in the city. With no separation of Church and State, virtually all aspects of civic life were carried out under the protection of one or more patron deities, and temples and shrines lay throughout the city, side by side with public buildings, workshops, and private houses (1). Evidence from the excavations of the Agora attests to the richness and variety of the religious life of ancient Athens; cults are represented by large temples (16), small open-air shrines (52), altars (2), and dedications. In addition, many of the small objects on sale in the market were decorated with lively scenes illustrating the numerous myths which tell the stories of the gods and heroes.

At the heart of the city, the large open square of the Agora was an ideal place for many of the festivals held in honor of the gods. The Athenian year was full of days set aside for religious activities. Though solemn in intent, these religious observances also provided an opportunity for good entertainment, with lavish processions, theatrical and choral performances, and athletic contests (3) making up an important part of every festival. In addition, the sacrifices of animals (4) provided a great deal of meat which was distributed to the citizens for large communal feasts. Thus many of the festivals took place in a holiday atmosphere, and the whole population would have partaken of the religious life of the city.

2. A youth sacrifices at an altar. Here the sacrifice takes the form of a simple libation; note the snakes, symbols of heroes, on the altar. Red-figured cup, 5th century B.C.

3. A torch race. Such races, held at night, are known to have been performed in honor of Athena, Hephaistos, and Prometheus. Red-figured pitcher, late 5th century B.C.

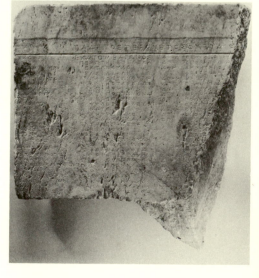

4. Sacred calendar. A list of festivals and the appropriate sacrifices (mostly pigs) for Demeter and other Eleusinian deities. Late 5th century B.C.

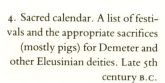

THE OLYMPIAN GODS

ZEUS

Zeus, father of the Olympian gods (5), was well represented in the Agora. A long colonnade, or stoa, was built along the west side of the square in the late 5th century B.C. and dedicated to Zeus Eleutherios (Freedom). Built in celebration of Athenian victories over the Persians, the building had handsome wall paintings depicting the twelve gods as well as Athenian military exploits (Pausanias, I.3.3–4). It was considered a suitable place for the dedication of the shields of those who had died in battle fighting for the freedom of Athens. An altar and statue of the god stood out in front of the building.

5. Zeus enthroned, holding his thunderbolt. Black-figured lekythos, late 6th century B.C.

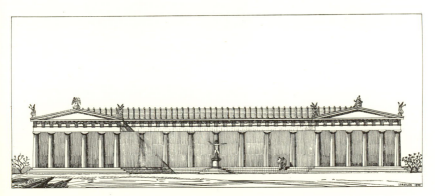

6. Stoa of Zeus Eleutherios, restored drawing. Late 5th century B.C.

Daughter of Zeus and Metis, the goddess of wisdom, Athena was the patron deity of Athens, having won the honor in a contest with Poseidon. She had three major temples on the Akropolis, but was not neglected in the lower city, where her aspect as goddess of arts and crafts made her an important figure in the Agora. She was worshipped with her father, Zeus, in both a small temple and the bouleuterion, and she shared the great temple overlooking the market square (16) with Hephaistos, also a patron of craftsmen.

7. Athena. The goddess usually appears fu armed, fitting the description of her in of the Homeric Hymns: 'dread is she with Ares she loves deeds of war.' Ror lamp, 3rd century after Christ.

8. Armed Athena; Panathenaic vase, 6th century B.C. This type of amphora served a specific function: to hold the sacred olive oil given as a prize to the winners of the athletic contests held during the Panathenaic festival in honor of Athena.

One side of the jar has a depiction of the goddess, the other a picture of the event for which the jar and its contents were the prize.

9. Demeter with Persephone, Iakchos, and worshippers. Votive relief of the 4th century B.C.

DEMETER

Demeter, goddess of vegetation and fertility, had her own sanctuary to the southeast, along the road which led up the hill from the Agora to the Akropolis. This sanctuary, the Eleusinion, served as a sort of Athenian annex for Demeter's great sanctuary and Hall of Mysteries at Eleusis, several miles to the west of Athens. Only partially excavated, the Eleusinion had a high enclosure wall, a stoa, and a temple. Numerous kernoi, special ritual vessels used in the rites of Demeter, were found in the area (10, 11).

10. Bronze token with kernos and ears of wheat, 3rd or 2nd century B.C.

11. Kernoi, small ritual vases, from the Eleusinion. 4th century B.C.

7

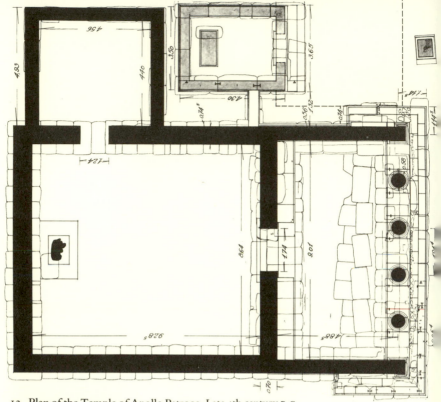

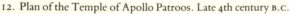

12. Plan of the Temple of Apollo Patroos. Late 4th century B.C.

13. Apollo, perhaps by the sculptor
Euphranor, 4th century B.C.

APOLLO

Apollo, god of light and music, was worshipped in the Agora as Apollo Patroos (Fatherly), the paternal deity of all Athenians as the father of Ion, founder of the Ionian race. His temple, a small structure of the 4th century B.C., lies just south of the Stoa of Zeus. A huge statue of the god, wearing the robes of a musician, was found near by and can perhaps be identified with a famous statue seen by Pausanias in the temple (13). It corresponds also to a description of the god in a Homeric Hymn: 'Apollo plays his lyre well, stepping high, and a radiance shines around him, the gleaming of his feet and well-woven tunic.'

14. Apollo and Artemis. Black-figured vase, 6th century B.C. 'Tall to look on, enviable in form, Artemis who delights in arrows, sister of Apollo' (Homeric Hymn).

ARTEMIS

Artemis, sister of Apollo (14) and goddess of the hunt (15), was worshipped in Athens as the goddess of good counsel, a useful deity in view of the often chaotic nature of Athenian democracy. A decree in honor of the people of Ephesos, a city where the worship of Artemis was paramount, was to be set up 'in the Agora beside the altar of Artemis Boulaia' (I 2361). Another inscription (I 787) records that sacrifices were offered to her before every meeting of the Athenian assembly.

15. Artemis in hunting garb, with dog, bow, quiver, and torch. Relief of the Roman period, deliberately mutilated.

16. The Hephaisteion. Second half of the 5th century B.C.

HEPHAISTOS

Sing, clear-voiced Muse, of Hephaistos, famed for inventions.
With bright-eyed Athena he taught men glorious crafts.

Homeric Hymn

The god of the forge was honored at Athens in the large Doric temple which crowns the hill west of the Agora (16), perhaps the most monumental temple erected to Hephaistos in the ancient world. The area around was found to be full of bronze-casting pits and other examples of industrial activity, suggesting that those who worshipped the god toiled near by.

17. Hephaistos. Note the work cap torch. Torch races were part of god's festival. Lamp of the Roman riod.

10

APHRODITE

The goddess of love was worshipped above the Agora on the slopes of the Akropolis, where at least two sanctuaries to her are known. Her popularity in the city below is attested by almost 300 statuettes (18) which have come to light in the excavations. Her son, the winged infant Eros, often had a share in her cults and was a favorite theme for jewelry (19, 20).

18. Aphrodite. Bronze statuette, 3rd century after Christ.

20. Gold earring in the form of Eros. Second half of the 4th century B.C.

19. Gold earring in the form of Eros. Hellenistic.

11

HERA

Hera, consort of Zeus, was not overly popular at Athens; no major sanctuary to her is known, though a few small dedications and altars have been found.

21. Hermes. Red-figured cup, 5th century B.C.

HERMES

Hermes, as god of trade, commerce, and thieves, found a ready home in the marketplace. Recognizable by his kerykeion (herald's staff, or caduceus), traveling hat, and winged sandals (21), he was a favorite subject for Greek artists as messenger of the gods. As god of doorways, likenesses of Hermes were set up on tall square shafts in front of every Athenian house (22, 23). This conservative type of representation was a popular form of public dedication as well, particularly along the entrance to the Agora at the northwest corner, to the extent that that entire area of town was known as 'the Herms'.

22. Herm, 5th century B.C.   23. Herm, 2nd century after Christ.

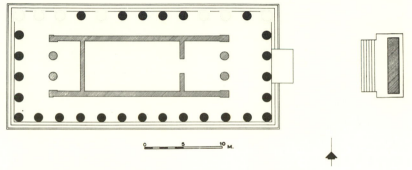

24. Plan of the Temple of Ares. Second half of the 5th century B.C.

ARES

A large temple of the 5th century B.C., similar to the Hephaisteion, was dedicated to the god of war in the Agora (24). It originally had stood elsewhere, however, and was dismantled and reassembled in the square only in early Roman times. The hill south of the Agora, the Areopagus, also bears the name of Ares, for it was here that the god was tried for the murder of Halirrhothios, son of Poseidon. The hill became the site of a venerable court of the same name which heard cases of intentional homicide.

POSEIDON

Poseidon, rival of Athena for the role of patron of the city, occurs infrequently at Athens, though he was worshipped with Athena in the Erechtheion on the Akropolis. His principal aspect, god of the sea, was celebrated by the Athenians in the magnificent temple which crowns the headland of Cape Sounion; parts of the temple, like the Temple of Ares, were moved into the Agora in the early Roman period. Poseidon's two other concerns, horses and earthquakes, were not particularly relevant to Athenian life.

HESTIA

'For without you mortals hold no banquet—where one does not duly pour sweet wine in offering to Hestia both first and last.' Despite the words of the Hymn, Hestia, goddess of the hearth, was perhaps the most neglected of the Olympians throughout Greece. She did not fare much better in Athens, though she was worshipped with Zeus in the bouleuterion. Her principal domain was east of the Agora, in the prytaneion (town hall), where an eternal flame was kept burning and where worthy citizens and ambassadors of foreign states were fed at public expense.

26. Satyr on a donkey. Red-figured
cup, 5th century B.C.

25. Dionysos with ivy leaves and his kantharos
(wine cup). Red-figured fragment, 5th century B.C.

DIONYSOS

Dionysos, god of wine, was worshipped in Athens south of the Akropolis
in a large sanctuary which included the theater, of which he was the
patron. In the Agora, Pausanias records having seen a statue of the god in
the Odeion of Agrippa. Also the patron of general riot and debauch,
Dionysos was a favorite subject for Athenian potters, and many drinking
cups were decorated with representations of the god and his tipsy cohorts,
satyrs and maenads.

27. Satyrs and maenads dancing. Black-figured cup, 6th century B.C.

Pan

Muse, tell me about Pan, the dear son of Hermes, with his goat's feet and two horns—a lover of merry noise...he sounds his note, playing sweet and low on his pipes of reed.
Homeric Hymn

Pan, the half-goat god of Arkadia, was worshipped with the nymphs in several caves scattered throughout Attica. In Athens he was worshipped in a cave above the Agora (title page), in appreciation of the god's help during the Athenian victory over the Persians at Marathon in 490 B.C.

28. Pan with his pipes. Roman lamp, 3rd century after Christ.

). Asklepios and Hygieia. Marble votive relief, 4th century B.C.

Asklepios

Asklepios, the healing hero who became a god, had a large sanctuary south of the Akropolis, next to the Theater of Dionysos, where he was worshipped with his companion Hygieia (Health).

HERAKLES

One of the most popular heroes of antiquity was Herakles (Hercules in Latin), the great strongman whose exploits inspired many representations by artists throughout Greece. So brave was Herakles that he eventually assumed the status of a full god, though it is his adventures as a mortal, particularly the 12 labors, which were so well loved. In the Agora, the labors were used to decorate the metopes across the front of the Hephaisteion, though the scenes have been badly mutilated over the years. In addition, according to Pausanias, a statue of the hero once stood near the Temple of Ares.

30. Herakles with club and skin of the Nemean lion. Marble statuette, Roman period.

31. Herakles wrestles the Nemean lion, his first labor, as Athena and Iolaos look on. Black-figured krater, 6th century B.C.

32. Altar of the Twelve Gods, Period II, late 5th century B.C.
Restored drawing.

THE TWELVE GODS

An altar to the Twelve Gods, perhaps, but not certainly, the Olympians, was set up in the Agora by the grandson of the tyrant Peisistratos in 522/1 B.C. (Thucydides, VI.54.6–7). Most of it lies under the electric railway, but the southwest corner of the enclosure wall and an early statue base (33) dedicated to the Twelve may still be seen. It was a common place of asylum for suppliants and refugees and, in one respect at least, was the heart of the ancient city. All distances from Athens were measured from the altar: 'The city set me up, a truthful monument to show all mortals the measure of their journeying; the distance to the Altar of the Twelve Gods from the harbor is 45 stades (9 kilometers).' From a milestone of the 5th century B.C. (*I.G.* II², 2640).

33. Statue base: 'Leagros, the son of Glaukon, dedicated this to the Twelve Gods.' Early 5th century B.C.

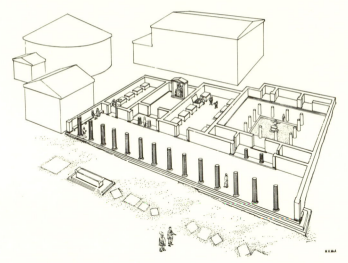

34. Metroon, the archive building and sanctuary of the Mother of the Gods, partial restoration. 2nd century B.C.

MOTHER OF THE GODS

The Mother of the Gods was the object of an imported cult from Phrygia, and one of the earliest of several foreign gods to find acceptance in Athens. By the 5th century B.C. she was the tutelary deity of the bouleuterion (senate house), and from the 4th century her shrine, the Metroon, served also to house the archives of the city. Pausanias records that her cult statue was made by Pheidias, and numerous small copies in marble, showing the goddess seated in a small temple (naiskos), have been found all over the Agora.

35. Mother of the Gods. Marble relief, 4th century B.C.

HEKATE

The triple-bodied goddess of the crossroads had a shrine on the Akropolis, by the Temple of Athena Nike. The many roads which converged at the Agora were also suitable places for her worship, however, and several small marble representations are known from the excavations. As a goddess of the underworld, Hekate was also closely associated with magic. Curses, written on lead tablets, were often addressed to her and deposited in graves or dropped down wells.

36. Hekate. Marble statuette, 1st or 2nd century after Christ.

37. Hekate and magical symbols. Drawing on a lead curse tablet, 1st century after Christ.

Isis, Sarapis, Harpokrates, Anoubis, and other minor Egyptian gods seem to have been introduced to Athens in the 4th century B.C. by traders coming into Piraeus: 'Resolved by the People, to give the merchants of Kition (from Cyprus) the right to own a piece of property in which they are to found a sanctuary of Aphrodite, just as the Egyptians are establishing the sanctuary of Isis' (*I.G.* II², 337, decree of 333/2 B.C.). Once installed, the Egyptian gods enjoyed great popularity in and around the city. Though their shrines lay beyond the limits of the Agora, small objects such as these demonstrate Athenian interest.

38. Isis in the form of a lamp. 3rd or 4th century after Christ.

39. Anoubis, the jackal-headed god. Glass amulet, 3rd century B.C.

40. Sarapis. Marble bust, 2nd or 3rd century after Christ.

ABSTRACT CONCEPTS

By the Classical period deification of
abstract ideas and allegorical figures became common. Statues of Democracy
and of Peace holding the infant Wealth
are known to have stood in the Agora.
In addition, a large statue, perhaps of
Themis (Justice), stood in front of the
Royal Stoa, an appropriate guardian
of the religious and legal proceedings
which were carried out in the building.

41. Colossal statue of Themis(?) which stood before the Royal Stoa. Late 4th century B.C.

42. Democracy crowns the seated figure of Demos
(The People of Athens). Relief above a law
against tyranny, 4th century B.C.

43. Goddess Nike (Victory),
recognizable by her wings,
sacrificing at an altar. Red-
figured pitcher, 5th century
B.C.

21

Beginning in the Hellenistic period with Alexander the Great and
continuing into the period of the
Roman emperors, it became cus-
tomary to treat rulers as gods,
often during their lifetimes and
almost always thereafter. No
fewer than 94 altars, for instance,
are known to have been dedicated
in Athens to the Roman emperor
Hadrian, who was particularly
fond of the city.

44. Cuirassed statue of the Emperor
Hadrian (A.D. 117–138); Athena
stands on the wolf of Rome.

45. Statue base of the divine Emperor Trajan (A.D. 98–117): 'Emperor Nerva Trajan Caesar
Augustus Germanicus (by) his chief priest Tiberius Claudius Atticus Herodes, of Marathon.'

HEROES

In addition to the Olympian and other gods, the Athenians worshipped a large assortment of lesser deities, demi-gods known as heroes. These were generally beings who were thought to have lived on earth and through special valor or other admirable qualities came to be regarded as divine after their death. The popular cults of heroes, like those of many of the saints today, seem often to have had far greater appeal than the official state cults represented by the monumental temples on the Akropolis. The citadel would be visited only a few times each year by the average citizen, whereas the small shrines and sanctuaries of the lower city were far more accessible and were frequented with far greater regularity.

THESEUS

One of the legendary founders of the city of Athens, Theseus was the most beloved of Athenian heroes, something of a rival of Herakles, the great Peloponnesian hero. His center of worship was a large sanctuary east of the Agora which contained his bones, recovered from the island of Skyros by Kimon in 476/5 B.C. Within the Agora he was depicted on large wall paintings in both the Stoa Poikile and the Stoa of Zeus, sculptures of the hero adorned both the Royal Stoa and the Hephaisteion (47), and a statue of him stood near the Temple of Ares.

46. Theseus and the Minotaur. Athenian bronze coin, 3rd century after Christ.

47. Theseus fights the bull-headed Minotaur. Metope of the Hephaisteion, 5th century B.C.

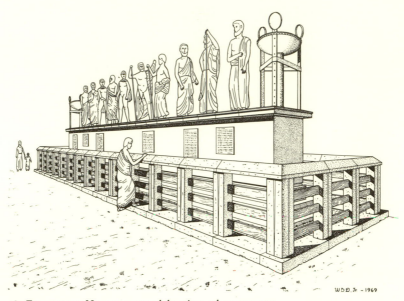

48. Eponymous Heroes, restored drawing. 4th century B.C.

THE EPONYMOUS HEROES

With the foundation of the Athenian democracy at the end of the 6th century B.C., the entire citizen body was divided up into ten new tribes, the basic political units of the new government, designed to replace the four Ionian tribes. Each of the new tribes was named after an early Athenian hero. To ensure a proper choice, the names of 100 Athenian heroes were sent up to Apollo's oracle at Delphi and ten names were selected: Hippothoon, Antiochos, Ajax, Leos, Erechtheus, Aigeus, Oineus, Akamas, Kekrops, and Pandion. Each of these tribal heroes had his own sanctuary and sacrifices somewhere in the city. In addition, they were represented together in the Agora, on a long monument displaying bronze statues of all ten heroes. The base of this monument served as a public notice board, and beneath each tribal statue would be posted notices relevant to the members of that tribe: military conscriptions, proposed legislation, public honors, impending lawsuits, and the like. This important monument stood in a prominent position within the Agora square, just across the street from the Metroon (34) with its collection of more permanent records.

24

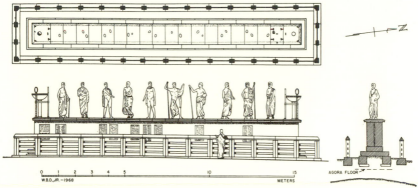

49. Eponymous Heroes, restored drawing. 4th century B.C.

In later times, when the Athenians wished to honor a foreign ruler, the highest honor they could bestow was to name him an Eponymous Hero. This honor was paid to the Macedonian king Antigonos and his son Demetrios, to Attalos of Pergamon, Ptolemy of Egypt, and the Roman emperor Hadrian (50).

50. Base for the monument of the Eponymous Heroes. Note extension in foreground for the addition of the statue of Hadrian.

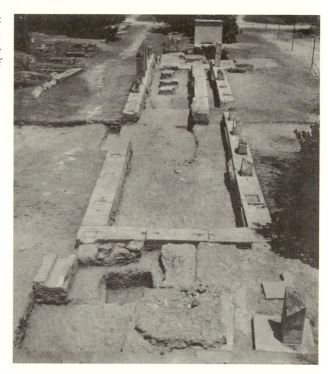

51. Fragment of the base of the Tyrannicides monument. Most of the name of Harmodios (ΑΡΜΟΔΙΟ) can be read in the top line. Probably from the second pair of statues, 477 B.C.

THE TYRANNICIDES

In 514 B.C. two men, Harmodios and Aristogeiton, killed Hipparchos, one of the two tyrants ruling Athens at that time. When his brother Hippias was overthrown several years later, Harmodios and Aristogeiton were honored as heroes, and bronze statues of the tyrant slayers were set up in the middle of the Agora. These originals were taken by Xerxes during the capture of Athens by the Persians in 480 B.C. and a second pair was set up in 477. A century and a half later Alexander the Great sent back the original pair from Persia, and both sets stood in the Agora. Roman copies of the statues exist in marble, but of the Greek originals only small parts of the base have been found (51).

OTHER HEROES AND UNIDENTIFIED SHRINES

Numerous other heroes are known from the ancient sources to have been worshipped in and around the Agora, though their shrines have not been identified with certainty: Eurysakes, the daughters of Leos, Epitegios, Strategos, and Iatros. On the other hand, several small sanctuaries or cult spots that cannot be associated with certainty with any known deity have come to light in the excavations.

Many of these lesser hero cults seem often to owe their origins to the chance discovery of an early grave. Before the laying out of the Agora, the area was used extensively from the 14th to the 8th century B.C. as a burial ground, and later building activity often disturbed these early tombs.

Best preserved of the unidentified shrines is a small square enclosure at the northwest corner of the Agora (52). Square in plan and measuring

52. Crossroads enclosure with votive pots as found. 5th century B.C.

about three meters to a side, the sanctuary was an abaton, not to be entered. Chest-high walls of limestone slabs allowed the devout to look in, but not to go in. Within, there was an outcrop of hard bedrock, and on this stone dozens of cups and vases had been broken and left as offerings to the deity in the 5th and 4th centuries B.C. None of the dedications carry the name of the recipient, unfortunately, and the owner of the shrine remains a

53. Votive cup from crossroads enclosure.

54. Votive pots from crossroads enclosure.

27

55. Boundary stone of the triangular shrine at the southwest corner of the Agora: '(boundary)
of the shrine.' 5th century B.C.

matter of conjecture. One possible identification is as the Leokoreion, the
sanctuary of the daughters of Leos, who were sacrificed to save the city in
time of plague and famine and who are known to have been worshipped
somewhere in northwest Athens.

Another small shrine stood at the crossroads of the southwest corner of
the Agora (1). It was triangular, with a small boundary stone set at the
corner (55). A variety of offerings suggest that the cult goes back to the 7th
century B.C., though the boundary stone and the handsome polygonal
masonry of the walls of the shrine date to the 5th century B.C.

Several more minor cult spots are known, one lying just south of the
Altar of the Twelve Gods and another just west of the Panathenaic Way,
where a stone-lined cham-
ber was found containing
offerings of the 7th to 5th
centuries B.C.

Other heroes are known
from dedications alone. The
hero Kallistephanos (Well-
crowned), for instance, was
the recipient of a handsome
relief dedication by the cobbler Dionysios (56), showing the whole family hard at
work making sandals in their
shop.

56. Votive relief dedicated to the hero Kallistephano
Dionysios the cobbler. 4th century B.C.

28

57. Banqueting hero. 'Chryse to the hero.' 4th century B.C.

58. Inventory of a hero's property. 3rd century B.C.

A common way of representing a hero was to show him at a banquet, reclining and feasting on a dining couch. An inscribed inventory found in the Agora lists the equipment used for ritual dining in honor of such a hero: '(Property) of the hero: double-headed couch, mattress, bedspread, smooth rug, multicolored pillows 4, red cloth, linen cloth, the following silver objects: kylikes (drinking cups) 10.'

29

The site of the earliest syn-
agogue in Athens is not
known, but a possible can-
didate of the 5th century after
Christ would be the two
northern rooms of the Me-
troon, which were refur-
bished at this time. A small
marble plaque decorated
with a menorah (seven-
branched candlestick) and
palm branch (59) was found
near by.

59. Marble plaque with menorah
and palm branch. Late Roman.

CHRISTIANITY

The Athenians throughout the ages were
receptive to new gods and their cults. Dionysos was an import of the 6th century
B.C., as were Asklepios and Bendis in the
5th. Later the Egyptian gods and a wide
array of Eastern deities such as Mithras
were accepted in an enviable atmosphere
of religious freedom. In their religious in-
dulgence, the Athenians included in their
worship altars dedicated to 'unknown
gods' so that no deity might be offended by
human neglect.

Such open traditions were difficult to
put aside, and paganism died hard at Athens. St. Paul (65) had little success in his
mission to the city, and as late as A.D. 395,
according to the Athenians, the city was
saved from Alaric and his Visigoths by the
appearance of Athena and Achilles striding

60. Lamp with cross, 5th century a
Christ.

30

61. Lamp with chi-rho symbol of
Christ, representing the first two
letters of his name in Greek. 4th
century after Christ.

62. Lamp with St. Peter, 5th
century after Christ.

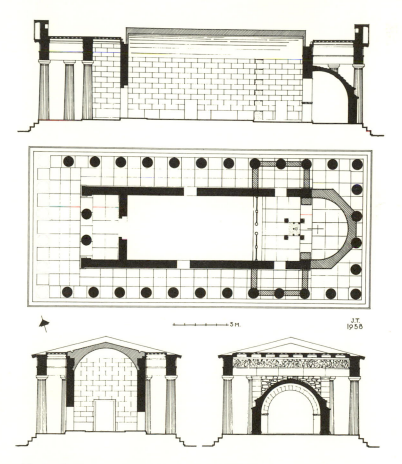

63. The Hephaisteion, converted into a church of St. George. 7th century after Christ.

64. Church of the Holy Apostles, about A.D. 1000.

65. Saint Paul. Lamp of the Roman period.

fully armed on the walls of Athens. Christianity seems not to have gained the upper hand until the 6th century after Christ, and only then with imperial help. In A.D. 529 the Emperor Justinian forbade any pagan to teach philosophy at Athens and this proved the death knell of the old religion. Pagan sculpture was mutilated (title page, 15, 47) and Christian symbols became increasingly common (60–62). Some of the old temples were converted into churches, including the Hephaisteion (63); others were torn down and great basilicas were erected over their ruins. Twelve churches were founded in the area of the present excavations and one—the Holy Apostles—has been restored and stands today, a final reminder of the long progression of gods and heroes worshipped in the Agora of Athens.